High in a tree lived a family of little brown birds.
They were Father Bird, Mother Bird and Little Bird.

"Just watch me!" trilled Father Bird, doing his finest acrobatics … for the tenth time.

You see, Little Bird simply would not fly.

"Lots of birds don't fly," he said.

Little Bird looked down at the duck pond.
The ducks didn't fly very much, he knew.

"Oh, but we swim and dive!" quacked
a friendly duck. "Look!"

The duck bobbed her head under the water.
"Ugh!" said Little Bird. "I don't want to
get my feathers wet!"

"Lots of little creepy-crawly creatures can't fly," insisted Little Bird.

But lots of them could!

"I've never seen the old owl who lives in a hole in our tree flying," cried Little Bird.

The owl opened his eyes. "I fly at night on silent wings," he hooted, "looking for my supper!"

"It isn't hard to fly,"
whispered a beautiful butterfly.
"You just flutter your wings like this!"

Little Bird hopped down from his tree.

"I just don't NEED to fly," he cried.
"I can simply walk and hop about
with my friends."

It was peaceful in the long, green grass.
Little Bird felt happy.
There was no one to tell him he should fly.

But nearby, someone was creeping ever so slowly
towards him. Little Bird spotted him just in time.
Without thinking for a second ...

Little Bird flew!

"Hurray!" he sang. "Cats can't fly,
but little birds can!"